The World's Greatest Greatest Business Card

Share Your Story

and

Skyrocket Your Success

I0076405

The World's Greatest Business Card

Share Your Story
and
Skyrocket Your Success

Keith Leon S

YouSpeakIt
PUBLISHING
*The Easy Way
to Get Your Book
Done Right*™

www.YouSpeakItPublishing.com

Copyright © 2017 Keith Leon S

All rights reserved. No part of this book may be reproduced or transmitted in any form or by any means without written permission of the publisher, except in the case of brief quotations embodied in critical articles and reviews.

This material has been written and published solely for educational purposes. The author and the publisher shall have neither liability nor responsibility to any person or entity with respect to any loss, damage, or injury caused or alleged to be caused directly or indirectly by the information contained in this book.

Portions of this book were previously published in *The Bake Your Book Program*, written by Keith Leon and Maribel Jimenez.

ISBN: 978-1-945446-33-7

Front cover photo by Alex Lowy
Alex Lowy's Photography Studio
www.LowyPhoto.com

Dedication

This book is dedicated to my mentors, Bob Proctor, Jack Canfield, and Dr. John Demartini. Thank you for all your support since the *Who Do You Think You Are? Discover the Purpose of Your Life* book project. You have been there for me so many times. I appreciate you and I cannot thank you enough.

Acknowledgments

Where do I even start to acknowledge the people who got me to where I am today? It would be a book itself if I thanked everyone.

First and foremost, thank you, Maura Leon, for your love, friendship, and for being the best business partner a man could ever wish for. You are amazing and talented. Your ideas have inspired thousands of people over the years. You are a blessing in my life and I thank God for you.

Timar and Aaron, you are my *why*! You are *why* I get up in the morning, my inspiration, my heart and soul. I am so happy to be your teacher, guide, and sometimes—I hope—your inspiration. You have grown up to be the most loving, talented, and incredible men. I am so proud of you both.

Thank you to Berny Dohrmann for showing me all the reasons to come to CEO Space. You encouraged us to come to the space with our then ghostwriting program. The fact that only one person in a room of over a hundred could afford to work with us was what took us back to the drawing board. It caused us to ask ourselves the question: *How can we be of service to all the people who really need a book, at a price they can afford?* Being in this question birthed our proprietary YouSpeakIt Book Program. This program has changed the lives of many entrepreneurs, coaches, consultants, functional medical practitioners, and visionaries.

Thank you, Shannon Burnett-Gronich and Ari Gronich, for being diligent and relentless about us attending CEO Space. We thought it was just another seminar and had no idea it would change the face of our business forever. Ari, you are a great friend and an even better brother. I appreciate you more than I can say in words. Shannon, it's so fun to create with you. I love attending and speaking at your Business Acceleration Summits. I encourage anyone who wants to take their own business to its next level and beyond to attend. Makayla Burnett, Alex Burnett, and Ryan Gronich, I love you! As I have shared with your parents, if you represent our future, then our future is in good hands.

Thank you to Ken Rochon at The Umbrella Syndicate for your friendship, and for all the incredible photos you have taken for our company.

Where would we be without our incredible YouSpeakIt team? Thank you to Maura L., Heather T., Nida P., Autumn C., Karen B., Alison D., Amy T., Bridget B., Jess S., Jody A., Sarah C., Kate L., Lily T., Peggy G., Melody M., Nancy C., Carole A., Patricia G., Rudy M., Sunni S., Rona G., Tina P., Steven E., Zulma J., Cameron

L., Maryna Z., Cathi S., Istvan, Katrina J., Ken R., Jess C., and Ben B.

A heartfelt thank-you to our financial supporters, Fred and Nita, Kat, Lin, Bradlee and Michael, and Wayne. Without you, the YouSpeakIt Book Program would not have been born and presented the way it deserved to be.

Thank you to our family for all your loving support and encouragement. I'm so grateful for how powerfully you root for us on each step of our incredible journey.

I must give thanks to all our incredible authors. We appreciate you for entrusting your story, mission, and message to us. We have loved and continue to enjoy working with you and watching you make a profound difference in the world. You make us incredibly proud. Every time we receive a proof copy of your book in the mail, it lights us up because we know your message will touch so many lives.

I love and appreciate my team of angels. You have kept me out of harm's way and moving forward for all my years.

Contents

Introduction

The *World's Greatest Business Card* is a title that I created eight years ago for a presentation. I discovered it sparks people's interest and opens a conversation.

What is The World's Greatest Business Card?

I saw a campaign years ago for a movie called *The Secret*.

The promotional trailer asked one question:

"What is *The Secret*?"

This trailer was so captivating, it was so good, that it left me saying, "I don't know. What is it? I need to know, what is *The Secret*?"

By the time the movie came out, we were all excited to find out what it was.

After a brief introduction, Bob Proctor, who is now my friend and mentor, got to answer that question.

He said, "The secret is the *Law of Attraction*."

Since I created The World's Greatest Business Card, it has reminded me of Bob revealing the Law of Attraction in the movie; now I finally get to reveal that the world's greatest business card is a book, and I love that.

This book is for you, if:

- You've thought about writing a book but have no idea where to start.

- You've started a book but something has stopped you.

- You've completed a manuscript and you're not sure what to do with it.

- You've written a book, and it's in print, but you have no idea how to use the book to leverage your business.

This book will help you with any or all these situations.

I am writing this book to share with you all the ways I know to succeed in writing a book, marketing a book, and more important, using a book as a launchpad for your success. I have tested these methods that I am presenting to you and proven that they work. I have taught them to hundreds — or by now thousands — of authors who are using these tools to write their books, to market their books, and to grow their businesses. I am writing this book because I have the experience and proof that the process I share with you will work for you if you do it exactly the way I teach you.

Let's face it, if you were clear about how to write a book, you would have written one already. If you knew how to move forward and get through obstacles and excuses, and plow through all of that to the end results, you would already have a book. And perhaps you do. If you have already written a book, congratulations! You know exactly what I am talking about right now.

If you have not written a book — or if you have, and you would like to use the book to leverage your business — I would suggest that while you read this book, you forget what you already know. Be willing to learn and stay open to trusting that I am the mentor who can support you to get to where you want to go. If you don't finish reading it in one day, make time in your schedule for reading this book. Most important, *trust the process.*

I hope that by reading this book you will:

- Gain clarity about where to start.

- Put into practice tools that will keep you moving.

- Discover ways your book can leverage your mission and your message into the world to grow your business, if that is your goal.

And if, after learning all of this, you decide you don't want to write the book, you will become clear about how to move forward in another way.

CHAPTER ONE

Why A Book Is The World's Greatest Business Card

WRITING A BOOK SETS YOU APART

Your book has become The World's Greatest Business Card: People are impressed because you have a book. They are blown away by receiving your book without having to pay for it. More important, they will never throw it away.

You give your book to them with a free offer they can't refuse, and it is only a matter of time before you hear from them. You *will* hear from them. You'll do business with them. This process is powerful. It has worked for many coaches, functional medical practitioners, spiritual advisors, financial advisors, and so on. It will work for you.

Five Advantages of Being a Published Author

Let's look at some of the benefits you gain by being a published author.

1. **Credibility** — By becoming a published author in a familiar arena, you position yourself as an expert in your field. You've taken the time to provide valuable information on a topic that benefits others, so you become a resource.

    Being published lends more credibility to your voice. Others in your area of expertise develop a belief in you that could otherwise take years to build.

2. **Respect** — You are a person who actually *did* write a book, not someone who said they would and never did.

    You have now identified yourself as a *doer* instead of a *talker* or a *dreamer*.

    You gain a level of respect by doing something others only dream of doing. It has been said that only 1 percent of those who say they want to write a book actually do. You instantly move into the top 1 percent!

3. **Clients** — More people will want to work with you than ever before. Being an expert in your field opens more windows of opportunity to get your name in front of potential clients, and will add credibility when you're a guest on radio shows, television programs, webinars, and teleseminars.

The quality of your clients will improve because you've positioned yourself as an expert in your field, allowing you to charge more for your work. As an expert, your clients will treat you as a serious professional and no longer attempt to get discounts for your valuable time and services.

With a book, your message reaches more people at once, more than you could reach by talking to each one individually. Potential clients have an opportunity to get to know you and what you're about, and then decide that they want to learn from you — all before they've met you.

4. **Raving Fans** — There's nothing more satisfying than meeting someone and hearing them share how your book touched their life, or receiving an email or letter from a raving fan. Your book will help someone journey to where they've always wanted to be, and they'll be grateful to you.

5. **Testimonials** — Once you receive these stories from people whose lives you've helped change for the better, you will have testimonials for your website, articles, proposals, bio, and for your next book. Each time a person shares how you've helped them, ask them to put it in writing, so you can share their inspiring story

with others. Everyone wins. It's a win for the author, the person giving the testimonial, and for the reader.

You Are a Doer, Not a Talker

Ninety-nine percent of the world are talkers and 1 percent are doers.

Ninety-nine percent of this world will sit around and talk about how *Someday* they are going to do something:

- Someday, they are going to write a book.
- Someday, they are going to climb that mountain.
- Someday, they are going to start their own business.

But those people will never actually do anything they say they will do. They'll spend their lives sitting around talking about Someday.

Now, if you get your calendar and flip through its pages, you'll see there's a Monday, Tuesday, Wednesday, Thursday, Friday, Saturday, and Sunday, but nowhere on that calendar is there a day called *Someday*.

Doers are the 1 percent. They are the folks who will actually do what they say they are going to do. One thing that will set you apart from everybody else in this world is if you actually do what you say you'll do. This makes you a doer.

I am going to assume that you are a doer because you have this book in your hand. The way you can prove to yourself and others that you are indeed a doer is to follow through and to write your book.

I encourage you to continue reading this book and to:

- Apply the things that you are reading to make plans.
- Set dates in your calendar.
- Follow up; do what you wrote on the calendar.

Clearly, You Must Be Successful

Once you have completed your book, it becomes your business card or launchpad to whatever you want to achieve—free promotions, such as written press, TV appearances, radio interviews, and so on.

And when you make a gift of your book, people will think: *Clearly, you must be successful if you can afford to give away something with a perceived value of twenty dollars.*

And if you hand it to them in the exact way that I teach you, with an offer that they can't refuse, you are really offering them a ton of value without asking them for anything.

Clearly, you must be a doer if you have completed your book.

Clearly, you must be successful if you can hand them a book with an approximate value of twenty dollars plus an offer and not flinch.

Does that make sense?

You are *giving instead of asking* from the moment you meet them, so clearly you must be successful!

WHY YOU WILL HEAR FROM YOUR POTENTIAL CLIENTS

Once you hand a potential client your book as your business card, you can count on hearing from them.

Why?

Because nobody ever throws away a book.

I don't think I can say this enough: when you give your book as your business card, it's only a matter of time before you hear from the person you gave it to. The question is not *if* you will hear from them, it's *when* you will hear from them. If you present your book correctly with an offer they can't refuse, that offer will harass and inspire them until they call you.

You will hear from this potential client because:

1. You have set yourself apart as a doer — you completed this book.

2. You are so successful, you can afford to give them a gift with a perceived value of twenty dollars like it was nothing.

3. You gave it to them with an offer that they can't refuse.

4. You established that you give first and ask later. This is very important in a first meeting with a potential client.

So, you have asked them for nothing, and you have given everything. You *will* hear from that person.

Use Your Book as Your Business Card

In the past, people would meet at a networking dinner or event to connect to one another. One asked the other for a business card, and the next time they needed the service of the person they'd met, they'd pull out the card and call. This was a way of doing business, and it worked. In the present day of cell phones, smartphones, and especially our busy lifestyle, this old-school way of doing business no longer works. Business cards are too easy to lose in the shuffle of a busy day.

Do you spend piles of money going to networking events, hoping to meet potential clients who need the service you offer?

Or perhaps, you hope to meet other likeminded people with whom to collaborate on future projects. You spend hours listening to speakers, missing sleep, and rushing through meals, all to go home with a stack of business cards.

How many of those business cards do you follow up on?

I have a personal rule: don't take anyone's card unless you're willing to follow up as soon as you return home, even if it's in the middle of the night after a three-day event. Even if you personally follow up on every card you take, you rarely, if ever, hear back from the person you reached out to after the event was over.

Many people will throw the stack of cards in the trash as soon as they get home and unpack. Some people are nice enough to put them into a tidy stack and wrap a rubber band around the cards. They'll hold onto this rubber-banded stack of cards until the next time they clean out their desks and, at that point, the cards go right into their circular file—also known as the trash can. It seems harsh, but think about how many times you have actually heard from anyone after you handed them your card.

Let's face it. Almost all business cards look the same.

Almost all business cards have the same:

- Shape
- Size
- Thickness
- Colors

Some may have a picture of the person who gave you the card, which is a step in the right direction, but it's not enough to keep you from tossing the card in the wastebasket the next chance you get.

When I hand someone a copy of our book, they feel honored. Most of the time, the person I give the book to will ask me to sign it. If they are a reader, they'll go home and read the book, getting to know me and my work in the world. If they aren't a reader, they'll go home and set the book down somewhere or put it on their bookshelf.

Then, the next person who comes along will say, "What's this book?" and before you know it, they're reading the book and becoming a fan.

Here's how you can change the outdated, typical scenario into a better one. Instead of tossing your card as soon as they get home, they now have something from you that tells them all about you and lets them get to know you personally. They may share what they've learned about you with friends and family. The worst-case scenario is they'll give the book to someone whom they care about, along with their highest recommendation, and you end up with yet another raving fan.

Your book is your card; it sets you apart from your competition and positions you as an expert. There is enough recognition for everyone, so I don't play the competition game. Instead, I take steps that set me apart from others doing similar work. I like to be the very best at what I do, and I am highly invested in providing value for my customers.

I believe it's better to over-deliver than to under-deliver.

So, instead of handing out a card, hand out your book.

Do you give a book to everyone?

No. Instead, you can use a series of questions to identify your perfect clients. If, after answering these questions, you think the person is a match for your services, then hand them a copy of your book.

Additionally, you can carry an extra copy to give to a person who appears to be in the perfect place to use the book's content to uplift their situation. They may not be the best candidate to become a client, but could use the information or inspiration. You will know when to share your book with a person who needs it. They'll be grateful to receive it, and you'll likely hear a follow-up story from them about how the book came at the perfect time.

They Will Be Impressed

As I said previously, your potential client—or whomever you choose to give your book to as a business card—will be impressed.

First, they will be impressed because you completed the book; most people are still sitting around talking about how Someday they're going to write a book. You have actually completed it.

Second, they will be impressed because you are able to give them the book and give it to them with an offer that they can't refuse. Over the years, as I have used my book as a business card, people have asked me to sign it. I've had them offer me money for it.

And by the way, if somebody offers you money for your book, decline and say, "No, this is my gift to you. It is my business card."

One woman even kissed me for giving her my business-card book. Now when is the last time that you handed somebody that teeny, tiny, piece-of-paper business card and they kissed you in return?

It's extraordinary when you hand somebody a completed book that represents who you are, what your business is, and not only what you do, but also *why* you do it. There's nothing more powerful to leave with a potential client than your book.

No One Ever Throws Away a Book

The great news about this book that you are now using as your business card, unlike the teeny-tiny piece of paper that somehow is supposed to represent your business, is that no one ever throws away a book. They will either go home, read the book, love you, and call you to do business, or they will throw it down on the table or stuff it onto a shelf. But every time they pass that book and they see it on the table or shelf, it says to call you and get that free offer, call you and get that free thing that you told them you would give them. It harasses them incessantly until they reach out to you.

No one ever throws away a book. If the book is good enough, if there's a fire they will run into the house to save that book. I have so many books on my shelf that I have not read for fifteen years—maybe I will never read some of them.

Do you think I would throw one of them away?

Most likely, I would not.

A client came up to me a few months ago, and he told me that he gave a book to a client who went home and put it on their table and didn't read it.

Their mother-in-law saw it and said, "What is this book?" and promptly took it from them.

A few weeks later, their mother-in-law called and set up an appointment and became a client. Not only did the person to whom the author gave the book become a client, but the new client's mother-in-law did, too. This is the power of a book as your business card.

EFFECTIVE USE MEANS SUCCESS

Since books have become the world's greatest business card, the first question that an event coordinator set with the task of promoting your business will ask you is likely to be, "What's the name of your book?"

Whether you're appearing on a radio, television, or web-based program, the producer will expect you to have a book. It's a given at this point, as part of the marketing designed to explode your business. If you want to go big, you've got to have a book.

The most successful ways for using your book as a business card have been proven to work exactly the way I am sharing with you here. Any deviation has *not* been met with equal success. On average, the people who have followed the methods I describe in this book have tripled their business within the next year. So, it's very important that if you're going to use the tools that I've taught you, you do it in the *way* that I have taught you. If you do this, you will succeed.

To Get to Larger Stages

You may be looking for opportunities to spread your message to larger crowds in person, on big stages, or at large events. Anybody who is running a large event is going to expect you to have a book, and when you send them your speaker proposal, they will most likely do their due diligence.

They are going to check for the items you wrote in your proposal:

- What does your website look like?
- What other events have you spoken at?
- Do you have a book?

Organizers of large events like to see that you have a book because it means that they'll have the opportunity to make some money from selling it at their event. They want you to bring merchandise and resources to sell, because their mission for holding a large event is not only to be of service to others and give them great information, but also to profit. You must show that you're going to be able to make them money before they place you on the large stage. They're more likely to offer the space and airtime to someone who can bring in a higher dollar amount. So, the two things you must have are a book and the ability to show them you can bring in the money.

You can easily turn your book into other programs and products by repurposing and repackaging the book. Examples of this would be as an Ebook, Kindle Book, Group Mentor Program, Personal Mentoring Program, Live Events, or Audio Book. This is now possible, because you've already done the heavy lifting, which was writing the book.

Good news: people do not get frustrated when you give them the same information in a repackaged format. They will thank you and appreciate you because most people need to hear something at least three times before it lands. Showing big-event coordinators that you do have a book that you've turned into programs and products that you are now able to sell increases your chances of speaking on the big stage.

Free Press, TV, and Radio

I have great news for you. TV shows, radio shows, and newspapers need content and they need it right now. In most cases, they needed it yesterday. The even-better news is that they are looking for experts to be on their shows.

So, what makes you an expert?

You are a published author.

You do not need to have the label "Doctor" in front of your name. You do not have to have any combination of letters after your name. If you are a published author, especially if you are a published author on the subject you are speaking about, you are now the expert. You've shown yourself as a doer, as someone who will complete a book.

All you need to do to get free press is learn how to present yourself and your book. When presenting yourself to producers of TV and radio, less is more. The less you can say, the better.

Here's a winning script for your call to a TV or radio producer:

Say, "Hi, my name is _____ and the name of my book is _____. I can teach your readers/viewers how to _____ in two minutes or less."

And then stop. Say nothing more. Wait.

The words that you used will tell them:

- I am a professional.
- I've done this a million times.
- I'm ready to go.
- I'm the one you want to have on your show.

You didn't talk forever and ever about your book, about how great you are. That mistake will make them hang up on you quickly, by the way. You told them only your name, the name of your book, and what you will do if they have you on the show. Now, all you need to do is be a great guest and follow up with a thank-you once you've completed being a successful guest on their show. Following up with a handwritten thank-you or some gesture will set you apart from everyone else. If you are already a great guest on the show, you will be the go-to person they'll call the next time they need an expert on your subject.

If Given Properly, You Will Hear From the Potential Client

In the past, when I met people for the first time, they would ask what I do, and I would talk their ears off. I would talk about all the things I do, and I would talk, and I would talk until the blood drained out of their faces.

Basically, they were looking around thinking: *How can I get away from this person who is using so many words?*

The way they'd try to move away was to ask, "Do you have a card?"

Sound familiar?

When this happens to you, it is the precise moment to set yourself apart from everyone else.

When they ask you what you do, you will tell them just two or three things:

For me, that would be, "I am a multiple bestselling author, a book publisher, and they call me 'The Book Guy'."

Their reply most likely will be, "What does that mean?"

Now is your chance to set yourself apart again, and instead of talking for the next ten minutes about what it means, you will come up with a statement like, "That means I can take you from wherever you are in your process to where you want to be."

To which their answer will be, "Do you have a business card?"

And you will say, "Yes, yes I do."

Now, hand them your book and say, "As you can see, I have clearly marked my contact information here," and point to where you've pre-stamped your contact info on the title page of the book. "So, when you're ready, give me a call and I will give you . . . ."

This is where you offer them that free thing that I've been alluding to, that item or service which has great value but has cost you nothing to deliver.

So, again you say, "Call me when you are ready and I will give you this free thing, which, by the way, has a value of five hundred dollars. When you are ready, give me a call; tell me that I gave you this book and I'll schedule your free gift."

Notice that I said "when you are ready" twice in that statement.

You don't want anybody to call you until they are ready. You will plant the seed, *when you are ready, give me a call and I will give you this free gift*. This wording presents your book properly. This tool I have just given you is invaluable! It will change your business forever, if you do it the exact way I just taught you.

Some people will be so blown away by you giving them a book that they will offer you money.

You will say, "No, this is my gift to you, this is my business card," which will blow their mind.

If you use your book as your business card, and give it properly without talking your potential clients' ears off, it's only a matter of time before you hear from them.

CHAPTER TWO

Why Most People Never Finish Writing Their Book

TALKERS VERSUS DOERS

As I previously stated, 99 percent of the people in this world are talkers. They love to talk. They will talk all day long—great storytellers, love to tell stories, and love to live in the past. And they tend to talk about how Someday they are going to do something.

The doers in this world are the people like the President of the United States, like Oprah, Jack Canfield, like me. We are the people who will actually do what we set out to do. We will set goals and we will accomplish those goals. We will make our listeners, our viewers, and our readers more important than the little liar voice inside our head that says we can wait until Someday. We will take the action items needed, set the appointments, and make ourselves, and our listeners, clients, viewers, or authors, as important as our family, as everything else. We will give the time needed to our project to make sure that it will come to fruition.

"Someday" and Acting-As-If

Have you heard somebody tell you that *Someday* they are going to write a book?

Or Someday they are going to do something?

Did you actually see them do it?

Here is the reason: Someday is not a day on the calendar. Someday never arrives.

If you'd like to achieve something, set a date and a time on your calendar and commit to yourself that on that specific date and time you will do that thing, or at least take the first step toward completing that action. When you set clear dates and times and commit to keeping your promise to yourself, you'll accomplish the goals you have created before you know it.

There's a term that people throw around, called *acting-as-if.*

There is a huge difference between somebody who acts rich when they aren't, meaning they present themselves as an expert who can teach you how to become rich, when they are driving the Pinto, right?

That's the type of acting-as-if that I would not personally agree with or condone.

To clarify, when I say act-as-if, I'm talking about more of an affirmation or a declaration to yourself. I believe that if you tell yourself something enough times and long enough, and you are consistent with this, it will retrain your subconscious mind to believe that it's possible, or it will create a physical manifestation of what you've been saying. And sometimes, in some cases, both will happen.

How can you do this?

1. Find a goal—something you have not done before that you want to do.

2. Write down that goal in a very short sentence *as if* it has already happened.

3. Post it in a place where you'll see it often—the bathroom mirror, the dashboard of your car, on your nightstand.

4. Repeat it to yourself out loud as often as possible.

You could post it in several places. Repeat that goal. It will come to pass.

Following are a few examples.

You can set a goal to **create financial abundance in your life**, and turn it into affirmations like:

- I am financially abundant.

- People value the work I do, and they are happy to pay me what I am worth to do it for them.

- Money comes to me easily and frequently.

- Abundance is mine and I am grateful.

You can set your goal to create better relationships.

- Every relationship I have is a relationship with myself.

- I love myself and treat myself with respect.

- I attract only those who see my value.

- I am now attracting those who are a perfect match for my energy.

- I am open and willing to share my heart with others.

Once you have set this affirmation or declaration and repeat it to yourself over and over again, part of you will start to believe it. Then you'll discover that without even thinking about it, you're presenting yourself as if it has already come to pass, *a done deal.* Maybe your chest sticks out just a little bit more or you stand up a little straighter when you are sharing with somebody about what you do. Or you're feeling like it is coming to fruition. When I say *act-as-if*, I mean put yourself in that place of having already achieved it.

Tell yourself that you can and you will achieve it. Back it up with action, and it will not be long before you have it.

Doers Do; They Don't Talk

According to *USA Today*, 82 percent of adults dream of writing a book. That means eight out of ten people want to write a book, but in my experience, fewer than 1 percent will.

Let's divide people into two categories for just a moment.

First, we have people who talk about doing something, but will never do it. We'll call them *Talkers*.

Do you know anyone like this in your life?

Has this been you in the past?

Talkers talk a good game. They can make it sound like they are going to do what they're talking about, but will not take the actions needed to fulfill the words they speak. The challenge with this is, once a talker has a pattern of saying they are going to do something and it doesn't happen, over-and-over again, it's only a matter of time before you don't believe what they say.

It's only a matter of time before *they* don't believe what they say. It becomes a never-ending cycle of unkept promises.

Next, there are people who do what they set their mind to achieve, let's call these people *Doers*. Doers will do whatever it takes to fulfill the promises they make to themselves and others, as long as it's in their control. Doers set achievable goals and take the actions or the baby steps needed to reach their goals. Doers are the leaders of the world.

Do you want to be a talker or a doer?

This is the ultimate question for you to answer.

If your answer is doer, then start turning your ideas into accomplishments. You'll be in an elite group of people before you know it. You'll be in the 1 percent.

Doers recognize each other a mile away, which creates the opportunity to develop priceless connections with important people. Doers want to support one another as much as they are physically able to. This is why we see so many people in partnership with each other, such as Jack Canfield and Mark Victor Hansen of the *Chicken Soup for the Soul*® series, Ben Cohen and Jerry Greenfield of Ben & Jerry's™, and Michael and Rickie Byars Beckwith of Agape International Spiritual Center.

Doers Help Other Doers — Right Asking

When you are looking to get to your next level, whether in your business, your personal life, or your career, it always helps to have somebody who has achieved even more than you to support you in achieving your next step. A great way to do this is to reach out to a mentor, somebody who is super-successful in your area as you strive for success.

I used to be a champion of reaching out to these people and asking in a way that was completely ineffective. I would ask them to help me and in the asking I would talk their ears off. I would use too many examples and unfortunately, I would come off as somebody who needed them to get to the next level. I would appear needy. Of course, while it would have helped me to have their mentorship, support, or endorsement, I didn't *need* it. This realization was an important learning moment for me — I didn't want to present myself as someone who was needy when asking for support.

If you are in a relationship with somebody and they are extremely needy, what do you want to do?

You want to get away from them, right?

As quickly as possible, you want to get away from them. These incredible people felt this way when I was standing in front of them asking them for support in a needy way.

Over the years, I've learned what I now teach as *Right Asking*. I learned to ask in right ways. Right Asking is asking in a way that the person being asked can say yes, easily. They can say yes without having to do much work at all. If I am asking for an endorsement from them, it would be wonderful if I would provide three pre-written endorsement quotes for them to either choose one as is, change one a bit to make it sound more like them, or, write one of their own. If I show up asking this question and I make it easy, so easy that they could point at one and say, "this one" it greatly increases my chances of receiving a yes answer.

Right Asking is asking in a way that makes it so incredibly easy for that person to say yes that they will.

Doers love to help other doers. When you write down goals and achieve them, you leave a trail of success behind you. When you complete a book, you become an author. These are things that will present you as a doer. And when you stand in front of another doer, asking for their support in a way that doesn't feel needy and makes it easy for them to say yes, they will support you. Doers love to support other doers.

OBSTACLES

We live incredibly busy lives, with:

- So many things to do
- So many emails to reply to
- So many phone messages to return
- So many people pulling at us asking us to do things for them
- So many needs from our families

So many more daily tasks could go on this list. These are the things that can get in the way of writing your book. These obstacles, when seen as obstacles, will keep you from writing. We must realize that all these things coming at us are just *part of life*. They are *what is*, if that makes sense. Obstacles are going to be there.

The real question is: How can we live with these obstacles and still achieve what we want to achieve?

Excuses, Excuses, Excuses

There will always be other needs that feel more important than writing, especially if this is your first book. Writing your first book can be especially challenging. You've not yet developed the muscle that it takes to write and keep commitments to yourself to keep your writing appointments.

Many situations will tempt you away from your writing:

- A great party that you can go to
- A date that you can go on
- An open time when you can connect with your family and your children

These are all great things. But none of these activities will bring your book to completion.

I've taught thousands of people over many years how to write their books. I have heard a myriad of excuses over and over again. People have argued for their excuses and why it was okay that they did not keep their commitment to themselves or potential future readers by making these excuses.

Once you have made the choice to write your book—whether it is for you or for the person who is going to read your book—either of these, hopefully, will get you past all the excuses. My hope is that my bringing your attention to this right now will help you to notice the difference between an excuse and something that really requires you to stop your writing.

The one thing you can interrupt your promised writing time for would be a family emergency.

What constitutes a family emergency?

Somebody is bleeding and needs to go to the hospital. Once you have committed to your writing time and sat down to do it, anything other than something as drastic as that is in the category of an excuse.

Rate your commitment between the numbers one and ten. One being, "I'm not committed and will never do this," and, ten being, "I will do what it takes to keep my commitment no matter what it takes. Only a family emergency will stop me from writing at the scheduled time."

What number are you?

If you are not a ten, what would it take for you to be a ten?

Limiting Beliefs and Fears

So, what has kept you from being a doer in the past?

There are ten common excuses or obstacles that get in the way and deter people from writing.

Do any, or all, of these sound like you?

- I'm not a writer.
- It will be too hard.
- It will take too long.
- Nobody wants to hear what I have to say.

- I don't know what to write about.
- I don't know where to start.
- It will cost too much money.
- I may never finish it.
- I'll write a book, Someday.
- I don't know if my books will sell.
- It has to be perfect.

Thoughts like these are called *limiting beliefs*. Somewhere in your life, something made you feel like you weren't good enough. Someone said you could never accomplish something, or that you'd never amount to anything.

Any of this sound familiar?

It may have been a parent, teacher, sibling, grandparent, TV commercial, an article, the media, or maybe it was you, yourself, who made these awful and untruthful statements.

The *truth* is this: When you put your mind and effort into it, you can do anything you want! *You* can accomplish anything you truly desire with some work and dedication.

You will need to face your fears. Then you can move forward. We all have fear, every last one of us. The only difference between you feeling stalled by fear and someone like Jack Canfield, Steven Spielberg, or Oprah

Winfrey is that they had fear and forged ahead anyway! They realized that *why* they were doing a project was more important than the fear that stood in their way. They didn't let their limiting beliefs take them out, and neither can you.

The end results of publishing your book and the lives your book will touch are more important than the negative voices in your head.

Let's take a good look at the limiting thoughts that may keep you from writing your book. We first list the belief, then look at the fear underneath. Finally, we share what we know is the truth. We can look at these thoughts from the outside, having experienced them ourselves. Since we're on the other side of these fears, we can share the truth behind the fear and beliefs.

Limiting Belief — *I'm not a writer.*

Fear — I won't know what to do. No one will read it. I don't have the experience or education needed to be a writer. I'll just mess it up. I'm afraid of success.

Truth — I used to believe this, too. I barely graduated from high school, and English was my weakest subject. I can honestly say that I forgot more than I learned in high school English. This is why there are editors!

A good editor will take your random thoughts, bullet points, and chicken scratches, clean them up and make you sound like genius. An editor will dot all the i's and cross the t's.

They will put the commas, periods, and quotation marks where they should be. Let me go on record right now as saying, "Thank you, editors, for making our lives so much easier!"

Limiting Belief — *It will be too hard.*

Fear — I won't be able to do it. I'll fail. I can't do it.

Truth — It's completely up to you how difficult your book is to write. In this book, I will show you ways to make it simple and fast.

The two things that keep it hard are:

1. Your belief that it will be hard.
2. Not getting started in the first place.

Once you start moving forward, momentum and support make it easy. As you begin to have wins like finishing a chapter, having fun writing, or asking people to read what you've written and receiving positive, encouraging feedback, you gain momentum and writing becomes a breeze.

You don't have to invent or re-invent anything; just write what you know and love. The key to finishing your book is to begin. Get ready at your mark. Once you hear the gun, hit the ground running until you cross the finish line.

Limiting Belief — *It will take too long.*

Fear — I'll never get it done. I won't have time for this with all the other things I'm doing. I simply don't have the time.

Truth — It is completely up to you how long it takes to write your book. How long do you want it to take? This is one of the first things to decide before you begin. Once you have a clear timeline, you know how long it will take. This allows you to chunk it down and divide time into bite-sized pieces or baby steps.

Limiting Belief — *Nobody wants to hear what I have to say.*

Fear — Look at all the books in bookstores. Why would anyone care about mine? I'm not an expert at anything. Why would anyone care about my story? I'm not good enough.

I'm not worthy.

Truth — No matter what you've been through, where you grew up, if you were rich or poor, happy or sad, you've learned valuable lessons along the way. Maybe you learned those lessons the hard way, but you're still here to talk about them.

My good friend Maribel struggled with this in her corporate background. She always felt like she had to keep everything to the point and strictly factual. Her belief that nobody cared what she had to say was a real stumbling block that she had to crush to move forward in a tremendous way.

We're all different and have unique gifts to share. We have creative ways of wording things that will attract a variety of people to our message. There's so much beauty in our differences. Maribel learned to embrace the things that set her apart and accept that not everyone will like what she has to say.

There's a great quote I'll paraphrase here, "I may not know every key to ultimate success, but one thing I do know is the key to failure is trying to please everyone."

Once you adopt this philosophy, it frees you up to embrace yourself and what you have to say.

Are you still asking yourself, "Who wants to hear what I have to say?"

The answer is simple: anyone who has ever been through, is experiencing, or is afraid they'll experience what you've been through will want to read your story. This world is a big place. I guarantee there are people who NEED to hear your story and how you made it through the experience. No one can tell it as well as you can. People need to know your story and will be inspired by it. They can only have this experience if you're willing to sit down and write it.

Limiting Belief — *I don't know what to write about.*

Fear — I'm not sure where to start. What do I really have to offer? I can't decide what to do. I need help, but I'm afraid to ask.

Truth — If you're alive, you have something to write about. There are issues you've moved through, or perhaps you've gained experience in your field of work. How will you pick one subject you know from your list? How will you know if your topic is Hot or Not? The answer is to write about something you know. That's it. Just write what you already know and you'll have a great book.

Limiting Belief — *It will cost too much money.*

Fear — I don't have enough information about how much it'll cost. The fear of the unknown is beating me right now. I don't know if it's less expensive to self-publish or pursue a traditional publisher. Someone will rip me off. I'm going to lose money.

Truth — I know exactly how limiting this belief can be. I faced these fears myself before I published my first book. The good news is there are many new and reasonably priced publishing options. Technology has brought an ease and grace to making these decisions. No matter what your budget is, there are options for you that make it easy to get started.

Start right where you are and build to where you aspire to be.

Limiting Belief – *I may never finish it.*

Fear – I'm setting myself up for failure again. I never finish what I start. This will take a long time. I can't do it. I don't have what it takes to complete a book.

Truth – If you don't start, you'll never finish. Getting started is the key! You need what I call a *Roadmap to Success*, which I will provide for you in Chapter Four. Having your roadmap in place will keep you from writing aimlessly and help you stay on course. Before you know it, your book will be completed and ready for print.

Limiting Belief – *Someday, I'll write a book.*

Fear – I'm not ready. I won't do it right. I can always put it off until later. I'm afraid to start writing.

Truth – Someday never comes. Someday doesn't exist. Here is how I combat this particular fear. I use a mathematical formula which goes like this:

Someday = Now

Anytime I find myself saying, "I'll do it Someday," I've agreed with myself that I will take a step toward getting it started, right then and there. Now is the time. Now is all we have for certain in this world. Reading this book *now* has moved you one step closer to writing your book. It's the first step on your path to being a published author. Congratulations on taking your first step!

Limiting Belief – *I don't know if my book will sell.*

Fear – How can I sell books if I self-publish? I'm not a salesperson. I don't know what to do. I'm all alone in this.

Truth – It's far too early to concern yourself with these fears. The objective is to write the book. You now have an expert on your team: me. I will walk you through the process. The only way to write a book is to get started. Don't let anything take you out.

What if you never sell a single book?

At least you wrote it. You're a *doer* instead of a *talker*, and you'll have the respect of your mate, friends, family, clients, coworkers, and most importantly, yourself.

Limiting Belief – *It has to be perfect!*

Fear – What if people don't like it? I don't trust that I'm already an expert. I need to know more about the subject. If writing is easy, I must be missing something. I'll make a mistake in how I present my material. I don't have the credentials to write about it.

Truth — There's no such thing as a perfect book. There are hundreds, if not thousands, of books on the same subjects, yet each one was written uniquely and resonates with each reader differently. The way you write your book will be exactly the way your intended reader needs it described and formatted to understand it best. If there's an inspired message in your heart, the way you write is exactly how it needs to be written.

The truth is you can only focus on one thing at a time. If you choose to focus on the people your book will help, the people it will inspire, and good it will do in the world, your limiting beliefs will show up far less often. If you keep your focus on the truth, you'll see the limiting belief for what it really is: a lie.

The time it takes you to return to the truth will become shorter and shorter until you make it through entire days without limiting beliefs. You'll start to string days together into weeks, and so on.

I'll be completely honest with you. I have had every one of these limiting beliefs myself at one time or another. The good news is that I didn't let it stop me. I faced my fears and wrote anyway. Developing the ability to overcome these fears led me to develop the *You Speak It* Book Program with my wife, Maura.

This process makes it so you don't even have to put pen to paper to write a book. Your commitment is just to show up to seven phone calls led by us, talk about what you already know, and we do the rest.

Did you know your new book is a lead generating tool?

In this book, I will teach you how to use your book to skyrocket your business, positioning you as the expert to attract lucrative opportunities and those who respect your work.

What You Don't Know Won't Hurt You

Over the years, I've seen so many people get taken out by the fear of the unknown, all of the fears and limiting beliefs behind the unknown. The truth is, what you don't know won't hurt you. Do research, find mentors who do know what you don't know. Once you have done your due diligence, make the decision that feels best to you.

As an entrepreneur, I have experienced the three Fs many times: I have Failed Forward Fast more times than I can count. For so long, I didn't want to take the slow road of experience. I always wanted to jump right to the top—right to the end! Because of my unwillingness to slow down and take one baby step at a time, I had what many people would call failures. I don't call them failures. I call them valuable learning experiences.

Once I failed forward by myself enough times, I decided to start reaching out to mentors. These were people who were already experiencing success in what I was working toward doing myself. I showed up as a *doer,* not a *talker*; practiced Right Asking; and these mentors took me under their wing and ultimately helped me become "The Book Guy." What I didn't know didn't hurt me, because it got me to humble myself enough to ask for support from the very people who could give me the support.

LACK OF TIME

For almost fifteen years now, I have heard people share what gets in their way:

- Obstacles
- Excuses
- Limiting beliefs
- Fears

One of the obstacles that comes up for most people is lack of time. We are all incredibly busy and there is so much to do. If you want to write a book, you need to do more than have the time to do it — you must *make* the time to do it. To get your book done, you need to make the time to write.

Working Full-Time in Your Business

Are you working your business, or is your business working you?

This is a question that I have asked myself many times over the years. I believe that every business owner should ask themselves the same question.

It's funny what people who don't own a business think of entrepreneurs and business owners:

- We're sitting on a beach drinking margaritas.
- We're playing a few rounds at the golf course.
- We're sitting at home in a giant pile of money throwing it in the air or counting it.

As a business owner, you are probably working more hours than you worked when you were an employee. As a business owner, especially when you start, you may be working fifty, sixty, seventy, even eighty hours a week.

Are you the type of business owner that is able to punch out at five o'clock and call it a day?

Or are you, like me, even after you punched out, sitting around still thinking of all the incredible ways that you can grow your business and things you need to do to expand your reach?

This is all understandable for a business owner. In order to have time to write your book—a very important, proven piece to growing your business—it is important to *make time* to write your book.

Working full time in your business is part of owning a business. At some point, you decide to delegate your tasks to someone else. If you are not at that point yet and you want to write your own book, it is important for you to schedule in the time and make your book as important as your clients.

Family and Community

Another thing that can get in the way of your writing is family members pulling at you. You are working long hours, you finally show your face, and the family wants to spend time with you.

How can you look at those sweet, loving eyes and tell them, "Oh, I just came out to get a glass of water, and now I need to go back and write my book"?

I completely understand this. Perhaps you are part of a church community and you are being of service and those people want your time; they want you to be working with them to grow the community. People pull on us from all different directions. Our time is our commodity and people want it. This is all completely understandable. We love our families. We want to spend time with them. And yet, this book that you want to write is going to support them, it's going to help them when you grow your business and you're able to phase yourself out of the busy work that you are doing. You will end up having more time for them in the long run.

Share with your family, church community, and social groups, "I am writing a book, I will be dedicating time to write this book. And once I am done writing it and it's in editing, I will have more time."

You may be surprised to find out that these people are excited about you writing a book.

They may ask you things like, "How may I support you? What can I do?" and when you show up as the person who completed writing a book, they will all be incredibly proud of you.

Other Obligations—Putting Yourself Last

I am here to be of service, I have known that since I was child. When I was a teenager and up until I started my own business almost fifteen years ago, every job that

I did was in the service industry. I've been all about service for everyone else my whole life. Because of that I always had a tendency to put myself last and to put others first. This carried over into my business once I started it.

I would tell myself and my family things like:

The customer is always right.

The customer comes first.

I have to take care of this client.

I'll be with you in just a moment, Son; I have to finish these notes for my meeting tomorrow.

Yes, Honey, we'll be able to go out to a movie sometime but I have to take care of this work now.

Yeah, that was me, until I realized that in order to get my book written I would have to make myself as important as all of those other people. It felt very strange to me, to put myself first.

I thought to myself:

- *What does that mean?*
- *What would that look like?*

For me, it looked like pulling out the calendar and writing in an appointment for writing time. Yes, I did it for me, but I also did it for the people I was writing the book for, the people it would serve. It took me scheduling that time and then taking it to the next level of commitment to myself and to my potential readers that I would keep the appointment, no matter what, short of a family emergency. I would keep this appointment.

I made the appointments. I kept the appointments. Truly, this is the only way I was able to get my book done. I suggest that in order to get your book done, you do the same.

CHAPTER THREE

Traditional Publishing Versus Self-Publishing

TRADITIONAL PUBLISHING IN THE CURRENT MARKET

There are many different publishing options available for authors today. In this chapter, I focus on the two most common options available after your book is written: either sell it to a publisher to produce, market, and distribute the book, which is the traditional method, or sell it yourself. For now, let's have a look at traditional publishing.

It's Not What It Used to Be: What It Really Is

Every time I watch a Woody Allen movie, or any movie that focuses on authors and the traditional model, I want to shout out loud, "No, you're misrepresenting how it really is!"

The model portrayed in the movies doesn't exist anymore. There are only a handful of Big House traditional publishers left.

Why?

Because they're still trying to do it the old-school way in a new-school world. Maybe they haven't noticed that print ads are out of style, and digital and social marketing is the way to survive in the current market. Perhaps they didn't know that Kindle books and other digital formats outsold printed books in the last few years. There is a misconception that book signings will sell enough books to pay for a flight, hotel, and food for the author. It's an incredibly enticing fantasy that's still being portrayed.

The truth is that a Big House traditional publisher (such has a HarperCollins) will not take on new authors.

If you got an agent to submit your manuscript and they loved it, you'd need to prove:

- You have a strong joint-venture marketing plan in place.

- You have the outreach to sell a ton of books.

- Your email list includes a hundred thousand people.

- You have a social media presence with followers at maximum capacity.

- You have experience doing public appearances, both live and recorded events.

If you had all of this in place, why on earth would you need them? To take all your profits?

Let's look at the definition of traditional publishing now.

In traditional publishing, you, as the author, would completes a manuscript, write a query letter and a proposal, and submit these documents to a publishing house. An editor would read it, consider whether it's right for the house, and if they decided to reject it, that would leave you free to offer it to a different publisher or to self-publish.

If the publishing house decided to publish the book, the house would buy the rights from you and pay you an advance on future royalties. The house would put up the money (which is a loan) to design and package the book, print as many copies as it thinks will sell, market, and finally, distribute the finished book to the public.

Advantages and Disadvantages

Some advantages of traditional publishing you may consider are:

- You're paid an advance on royalties, though it's usually only a few thousand dollars, sometimes less.

- You need to focus only on writing the book. After that, the publisher takes over most of the duties.

- Most marketing tasks are handled by the publisher.

- The publisher assumes the upfront costs of producing, marketing, and selling the book. This is a loan that will need to be paid back from book royalties.

Some disadvantages of traditional publishing you should consider are:

- It's time-consuming to create a proposal to pitch your book idea to publishers.

- The publisher may not be interested in your topic.

- Having your book made by a publisher can take a long time, because you may have to approach many, many publishers.

- You split profits and receive royalties on a fraction of the sales profit, usually around 10 percent.

- Royalties are normally only paid once or twice a year.

- Marketing is handled at the publisher's discretion. It may be spread thinly amongst other titles, so the publishing house's marketing department may not make a special effort to promote your book.

- Books accepted by publishers are usually longer and are required to meet an established number of pages.

- It's common to receive a large number of rejection letters, because only a small percentage of books are accepted by publishers.

Hesitance to Sign New Authors

Many authors choose to self-publish for two reasons:

1. There's a huge market for *Print on Demand* or POD publishers to capitalize on.

2. Traditional book publishers want to sign authors and books they believe will be a sure thing.

The chance of getting published through a traditional publisher these days is possible but rare. In this market, you write hundreds of query letters, mail countless chapters for initial review to agents, and then receive the, "Thanks, but no thanks. Don't call us, we'll call you," letter. Most likely feeling rejected and frustrated, you pull yourself up by the bootstraps, hone the manuscript once more, and write an even more intriguing query letter or proposal to the next agent or publisher, only to risk continual rejection.

After months of consistent effort, the rejections will get very frustrating and tiresome. The postal clerk now knows you by your first name, might comment on the agency or publisher you're sending the manuscript to, and automatically knows the postage it will take to ship three chapters anywhere in the United States.

How in the world can you, a new author, compete with a James Patterson, Stephen King, or John Grisham? You can't. All of these authors have long, successful careers and have sold millions of books. They're the cash cows for the traditional publisher.

Is it any wonder traditional houses are so hesitant to take a chance on a new author?

Well, new authors are taking matters into their own hands! POD companies have noticed there are literally millions of people who want to publish their memoirs, fiction, and nonfiction without having to go through the years of anguish over rejections.

We know we're laying this scenario on a little thick, but we want to make sure you're prepared for the road ahead, so you can truly decide which direction is best for you. Say hello to the world of self-publishing!

SELF-PUBLISHING IN THE CURRENT MARKET

Self-publishing has its benefits and certainly has its drawbacks. I will present both to you and you can come to your own conclusions.

What's the Process?

If you self-publish, you are responsible for marketing and distributing the book, filling orders, and running advertising campaigns. In the past, you'd have to decide on the number of copies to print, sometimes resulting in stacks of unsold books gathering dust in the garage! Fortunately, the Print on Demand technology now used by some self-publishing companies means authors can have fewer copies printed — only as many as they need — in fact.

Advantages and Disadvantages

Some advantages of self-publishing to consider are:

- You retain complete control of the look and content of your book.

- You can put as much time and effort into marketing your book as you wish. You may even do a better job than a publisher who is working on promoting numerous titles at the same time. You can take marketing your book one baby step at a time.

- You may be able to target a niche audience better than a traditional publisher.

- The book's page count doesn't have to be as long as a traditionally published book.

- You may already have an audience and can keep 100 percent of the profits.

- You don't have to sell as many books to make a profit as you would with traditional publishing.

- Sometimes well-received, self-published books are bought by big publishers.

- There is no storage space required for your printed books. As each one is ordered, a book is printed and mailed to the customer. No muss, no fuss.

- You can sell your book online with Barnes & Noble and Amazon.com, just like traditional publishers.

- You can have fast, easy formatting, book design, and other book services for a relatively low price. We provide all these services.

- You build immediate clout, because you have a book in hand, to sell.

Some disadvantages to consider:

- There's more work involved in handling the extra tasks of editing, proofreading, typesetting, cover design, and marketing to the public.

- You will pay all upfront costs of producing and marketing your book.

- An ISBN number must be purchased in order to sell your book in bookstores. You'll need to make sure to purchase directly from Bowker, and not get taken by agencies that purchase ISBNs and sell them cheap. Ultimately, these agencies own your book because they are the true owners of the ISBN.

- As the author, you must register as your own publishing company in order to receive an ISBN number, which can be time consuming.

- Just because your book is listed with Barnes & Noble doesn't mean it's going to sell a million copies and allow you to retire. Most people won't sell more than two hundred copies in their lifetime.

- You will do ALL promotion, including book signings, contacting news outlets, getting book reviews, and so on.

- If you don't hire professionals—like my company—to do the editing, layout, and book cover, your book will end up looking like a self-published book. There are choices professionals make in the editing and production phases that an inexperienced author will not know about.

For more information about self-publishing, check out sites such as:

- Selfpublishing.com
- Createspace.com
- Lulu.com

You Make the Call

What will work better for you?

Are you concerned about the process of creating and marketing the book?

Are you confident that a traditional publisher will pursue you to purchase the rights later, if you first choose to self-publish?

Which way is more profitable for you?

It's best to make a decision early, to prepare for what needs to be done before you write your book.

FUNDAMENTAL DIFFERENCES

Next, we look at the fundamental differences between traditional publishing and self-publishing.

Timeframe

With traditional publishing, a manuscript can take years to become a book. First, you may have to pitch the manuscript to several publishing houses before it's picked up, if it's picked up at all. Consider that bigger houses can take up to six months to work through the *slush pile*, the multitude of unsolicited queries on editors' desks, to get to your manuscript. Also, consider that you will likely have to approach several publishing houses before you get one to show interest. Well, you do the math—that's a lot of waiting!

If you have a literary agent, they can help you shorten the timeframe by leveraging the relationship required to get your manuscript in front of an interested editor, ahead of the slush pile. Then, if a publishing house does decide to publish your book, the actual process of producing it takes at least another year. Admittedly, this timeframe applies mainly to fiction.

Nonfiction books that are relevant to current world events might be pushed through more quickly.

With self-publishing, depending on the company, you can have a finished book, hardcover, paperback, or both, literally in your hands within six months. Of course, you have to pay for this service, which raises the issue of money.

Expense

With traditional publishing, you're paid an advance, ranging from small sums to seven-digit figures (if you are a famous, well-established author). Here, the publishing house, with its huge resources, experience, knowledge, and contacts, vigorously promotes your book. By contrast, in self-publishing, you could pay up to thousands of dollars, depending on the POD company you choose.

When you self-publish, you pay for everything:

- Designing
- Editing
- Printing
- Advertising
- Distribution

All of these steps are required to get your book into stores and ultimately into people's hands. You're all by yourself, so self-publishing works best for people who are good at self-marketing. The major payoff for all of your effort is control.

When you make use of a traditional publishing house, some of the costs may not be apparent up front:

- Bear in mind that an *advance* is really a loan that you will need to repay before you ever see a royalty.

- Every aspect of editing and production is also running a tab that you'll need to pay.

- You'll have to repay the publisher for any marketing they've paid for.

In total, by the time your book gets to print, you'll owe the publisher approximately $150,000. If you are only receiving a dollar a book, you'll need to sell 150,000 copies before you see any royalties from your book.

And, they better fly off the shelves quickly, or the publisher just may ship all the books back to you and send you a bill in the mail.

Control

Often, the joy of selling your manuscript turns into despair when an overzealous editor at a publishing house rips your manuscript into unrecognizable shreds. Publishers might refuse to publish a book, because it's too controversial, doesn't fit the house's list, or simply won't sell.

With self-publishing, you have much greater control over:

- Content
- Design
- Appearance
- Where the book is marketed
- Where the book is distributed

Having looked at the pros and cons of traditional publishing versus self-publishing, ask yourself some tough questions about what's best for you, your intentions, and your manuscript.

Are you willing to play the waiting game, because you hope to earn a large advance from a traditional publisher, or are control of your manuscript and quick turnaround most important?

The good news is that the available tools—POD, internet, and online booksellers—are leveling the playing field between traditionally published and self-published books. Authors now have more options.

Yes, writing a book may prove to be a lot of work, but when you hold a copy of the book that you're so proud of in your hand, there's nothing like it! It will be worth every obstacle you've faced, every excuse you've hurdled, and every appointment you have kept.

Portions of this chapter excerpted and paraphrased from speakingforaliving.com/on-demand-book-publishing, selfpublishing001. blogspot.com, and scribendi.com/advice/traditional_versus_self_publishing.en.html.

CHAPTER FOUR

How to Write Your Book

WRITE WHAT YOU DO, KNOW, OR LOVE

No matter who you are or what you've done until now, you have learned valuable lessons, skills, perhaps a trade, developed your sense of humor, and found ways to creatively express yourself. Whether you know it or not, you've learned something that other people don't know, but would like to.

What do you know really well?

Whatever your answer is would be a great subject for your book. The goal is not to reinvent the wheel, but to show people how to purchase, install, repair, or *be* the wheel. For example, if you're an artist who works as a waiter in a restaurant, you won't want to write a book on how to become a millionaire in seven easy steps.

First, if you work in a restaurant, you're probably not a millionaire.

Second, you have no story to support such a claim.

You could, however, create a book filled with pictures of your art and an explanation of what inspired each drawing. You could write a book about waiting tables and how to be really good at it. You could write a book for restaurant-goers about etiquette, such as tipping and how to order a steak the way they really want it cooked.

If you work at a corporate job in the personnel department, you could write a book called, *How to Hire the Right Person for the Job, the First Time.* This would prevent people from hiring the wrong person over and over again, which would save them valuable time and expense. A high turnover rate is expensive for a business owner. If you show how to save money by hiring the right person the first time, you'll be doing a great service.

I speak with many people who dream of writing a book, and a good percentage of them say, "Why me? Why would anyone want to hear what I have to share?"

My reply to that is, "Why *not* you?"

The only difference between you and John Gray, author of *Men Are from Mars, Women Are from Venus,* or Jack Canfield and Mark Victor Hansen, coauthors of the *Chicken Soup for the Soul*® series, is, even though they heard the negative voice saying, "You're not good enough. Who wants to read your book? Why you? You can't do it," they moved forward anyway.

If that voice pops into your head, just say, "No, thank you," and keep moving forward with your project.

It's most important for you to write what you know best. Your readers will feel it when you're sure of yourself. They know when you know what you're talking about. You can easily position yourself as an expert if you stick to what you know.

The world is waiting for what you have to offer. Once you become clear that you'd like to write a book, and know what you'd write about, every day that you don't write it, you're ripping off folks who would have benefited from reading it. By *not* writing the book you're doing a disservice to humanity. It's time to get started. You can do it! The world is waiting.

Flesh Out Ideas

A great way to flesh out ideas for your book is to take out a sheet of paper and list all the things you know how to do.

Which of these could you explain best?

This would be a great subject for your new book.

Sit down with a good friend or family member who knows you well and ask them to help you by saying, "Please tell me some things you think I'm good at."

You may be surprised at what they reveal about you. You may have never noticed how good you were at what is mentioned, or maybe you didn't even notice you did some of these things. Feedback from people who know you can be invaluable. Make sure the person has a positive attitude and knows the truth about who you are. You will get great ideas when you have the guts to reach out and ask for feedback.

Once you've brainstormed your list, spend some quiet time alone and ask yourself which things on the list you could explain the best. You don't have to write hundreds of pages on the subject. I'll show you a variety of ways to stretch your information to make a longer book. The idea is to have content that is rich and explained in a way that makes your subject seem simple and easily accomplished by the reader.

You can do it! Do it right now.

Take out a blank sheet of paper and list all the things you already know how to do.

Ask yourself: *which of these could I explain best in a book?*

Great job! You now have the subject for your new book!

Book Possibilities — Types of Books

I'm sure you're aware of the standard book possibilities, such as:

- Novel
- Life story
- Interview
- How-to

All these types of books can be written using the techniques I have shared with you thus far:

- Writing what you know
- Fleshing out ideas
- Creating your Roadmap to Success
- Creating powerful tools to make your book a reality

What I want to share with you now is called a **credibility book.**

If you're a business owner, consultant, fitness instructor, coach or service professional, you could skyrocket your business with a credibility book. Perhaps you've wondered how you can attract more clients, become an expert in your field, or raise your rates to an amount that makes you feel you're paid what you're worth! Perhaps you'd like to start a business and wonder how to build your platform, so once you launch your business, you have products to sell. Let's talk about creating a book using elements you have already created for your business. You can take those elements and turn them into a book that defines you as an expert in your field.

Here are five different credibility book creation ideas. See which one best fits your business.

1. A Book of Quotations

Use the internet, books on your shelf, or any source with quotations you like. Collect your favorites and put them into a book format. You can take the type of work you do and search for quotations that relate specifically to that subject or field of expertise. Let's say you're a life, business, or fitness coach. You could find quotations specifically about mentors or coaching. You can write an introduction and conclusion, add a few more elements, lay out the quotes, and you have yourself a book of quotes.

You could also compile your quotation book like a workbook. Put one on a page, include your ideas about what the quotation means, and give an action step so your readers can interact with what the quotation is about. You can also include space to write their thoughts if you want them to get more value from the book.

If you choose this type, be advised that there are specific laws regarding copyright and permissions for reprinting other people's work. As an author, it will be your responsibility to make sure you're following those laws and securing permissions, if necessary. Please read the article entitled, *When Do You Need to Secure Permissions?* at janefriedman.com/permissions/ if you plan to include anything in your book which has not been created by you.

Social platforms, such as Facebook and Instagram, are notorious for spreading falsely attributed or mangled quotations, so it's important to do your research before publishing that life-changing bit of wisdom. Make sure to check multiple, credible sources before believing it was Abraham Lincoln who said, "Don't trust everything you read on the internet."

2. A Book of Poetry

Do you have a whole drawer of poems or songs?

Maybe you're organized and have notebooks of them. Well, now it's time to share them with the world. You can take all of your written words and divide them into themes, for example:

- Love
- Beauty
- Nature

- Relationships gone bad
- Inspiration
- Frustration

Then make your Roadmap to Success (covered later in this chapter) with them. Once you have divided them into themes, arrange them in the order you'd like them to be. Then you can add an introduction, conclusion, some drawings or pictures, and a few more elements, and you have yourself a book of poetry.

3. A Book of Newsletters, E-zine Articles, or Blog Postings

If you've written a newsletter for your website, written e-zines or have a blog page, you've been writing your book for some time now and just didn't realize it. All you need to do is print out your previously written articles, lay them on the table or floor, and look at all the titles for themes.

Once you've identified at least three to seven themes, you can separate your articles into these categories, creating your Roadmap to Success once again.

Now, decide the order you'd like the stories to be in under each theme.

Once you've completed that step, decide the order for the themes.

Now, add an introduction, conclusion, some drawings or picture, a few more elements, and you have yourself a book based on your previous writings.

4. A Book of Photos

There are many ways you can approach a book of photos.

Review your pictures and ask:

Which would I like to share most?

Which do I like best?

Which photos have a story that can be told alongside them?

Which photos tell stories on their own?

You can create a book purely of photos and let them tell the story. You'll use your introduction to set up your story as you wish, and then write your conclusion at the end. You'll need a lot of photos for this type of book.

You can open a chapter with a photo, then tell the whole story behind the picture. If you do this, you can use fewer photos, but you will need to write a handful of compelling stories to go with them to fill up the space.

You can create a combination of these two styles, by telling a long story, but placing a picture every few pages that moves the story along, so all of the pictures relate to the story. There are endless possibilities with photo books.

You could display a photo and ask the readers to write their own stories on empty lines provided in the book.

Ask readers:

- What does the picture mean to you?
- What do you think the picture is about?

Then, you can follow that or include in a separate section what it's actually about.

Once you decide your approach to design your photo book, write your Roadmap to Success (described in the next section).

After you make the roadmap, lay out the photos in order, write your stories or ask all the questions about the pictures, you'll add an introduction, conclusion and a few more elements, and you will have a book of photos from your unique perspective.

Keep in mind, printing color photos in a book drives the cost up considerably. Make sure you have a market to purchase your book before considering it, unless you plan to use the book as a business card for your photography business and you're going to give copies away.

5. A Case Study Book

While you were in school, did you have to do any case studies?

Do you have a job or business for which you need or needed to do case studies?

Did you have to do one in order to put together your business plan when you were starting up your business?

If so, you may already have a case study book in your notes. You can bring all this information together in a way that will not only make a compelling book, but also position you as an expert in your field.

Once you lay out your case studies in the order you'd like to present them, using the *Roadmap to Success* technique covered later in this chapter, you will add some pictures or quotes, an introduction, conclusion, a few more elements, and you will have a case study book.

Discover Your *Why*

Discovering your *why* may be the most important part of the book writing process.

Why do you want to write this book?

Whom will you serve by writing this book?

Knowing your why is important because it is the thing that will pull you out of bed on the day that you do not feel like writing. It is the reason you'll make that appointment in your calendar. It is the reason that you will write, no matter what obstacle is in your way. When you know why you are writing this book — and more important, whom it will serve — you can begin to think of those people. And any time an obstacle or an excuse comes into your mind, remind yourself to see those people and think about those for whom you are writing your book. Think about how their lives may be served and how their lives may be changed if you keep that appointment for writing.

I have shared a process with thousands of people over the years that I'd like to share with you now. You can record yourself reading this aloud and play it back to follow the guided imagery, have a friend read it to you, or simply read a line, follow the direction with eyes closed, read the next, and so on.

> *Close your eyes and see your book finished, see it completed, see it in your hands.*
>
> *Now, in your mind's eye, hand the book to somebody standing in front of you.*

See how their face lights up when you hand it to them.

See that person coming back to you later at an event or at another time.

See them with tears in their eyes thanking you for writing the book.

Now see them sharing how much your book made an impact in their lives, or in some cases even changed their lives, or saved their business.

See it . . . and feel what it feels like. Take a few minutes to bask in the feeling of having inspired this reader to make changes in their life.

This is a great process, a closed-eye process that you can do to discover your why and any time that an obstacle comes up that you feel is more important than writing your book. Knowing your why is what will get you to write when you don't feel like it.

I like to say, "When your why becomes bigger than the lie — you have achieved mastery."

When I talk about the lie, that's the little liar that I spoke about earlier, that little voice in your head that says you are not good enough, you can't do it.

Say to yourself: *When my why becomes bigger than the lie – I have achieved mastery.*

And now you are back to writing your book.

CLEAR THE SPACE AND TIME

Previously, I have shared the importance of clearing space and time in your schedule for writing and keeping the appointment, keeping your word to yourself. Now, I want to share a few ways that you can get your book written once you clear the space and the time.

Writing in Short Bursts

One of the ways that you can get a book written without dedicating big chunks of time is by writing in short bursts. Some people are able to do this. I am not one of those people, but my previous business partner, Maribel, was really successful at writing in short bursts.

Maribel would set fifteen-minute appointments every day, five days a week — just fifteen minutes. She would take five minutes to think of her why, think of her client, do whatever she needed to get ready to go and then she would set a timer for fifteen minutes and write. She didn't judge or think about what she was writing; she would write whatever came to her mind about the chapter she was writing. She would write for fifteen minutes.

The alarm would go off. She would take a quick break. And if she happened to have a little extra time that day, she would come back and set the timer for another fifteen minutes. And then write some more.

Using these short bursts, she never felt like she had to commit a huge chunk of time or take away from her business or any of her clients. She just did her short bursts every day. Time travels by really fast so before she knew it she had completed her writing. You may want to try this and see if it works for you.

Marathon Writing

Marathon writing is the type of writing I prefer. If I am going to write, I will need to tell everyone that I love — all my clients, everybody — that I will not be available for the designated amount of time. Marathon writing is my time to *get my book done*. I am the type of person who would need to schedule a week or two to do nothing but write, because when I get an idea and I want to complete it, I want to get it done as quickly as possible with as much focus as I can.

The key to marathon writing is taking frequent breaks. Without taking frequent breaks you may run into what people call *writer's block*. I don't believe in writer's block. I feel that writer's block is nothing more than a pissed off inner child. Let that sink in for a minute:

There is a part of you who always wants to play and never wants to work. They are that child within you.

When you dedicate yourself to marathon writing you are saying to your inner child, "For this amount of time you will not be playing."

When you decide to follow through on this, your inner child may decide to retaliate. It may throw a tantrum to block you from writing.

You know what they say, "Hell hath no fury, like a pissed off inner child."

Honor Your Inner Child

The most effective way to never experience what people call writer's block is to honor your inner child. The way you can do this may seem odd to you, but rest assured that I have taught thousands of people this process. Many before you have done this, and many after you will do this.

We must treat our inner child as if it is our child. And the best way to continue to write is to keep our inner child happy so they don't throw a tantrum. Here's how you can do this.

Get a timer of some sort, some type of stopwatch, whether it be on your phone or a kitchen timer that dings, whatever you have, get yourself a timer.

Set the timer for twenty-five minutes and tell your inner child "Okay, writing is my fun, it's my time to have fun, so I am going to write for the next twenty-five minutes. And when this timer goes off, we are going to get up and do what you want to do for ten minutes. I will see you then."

And get to writing.

When the timer goes off, if you are writing by hand with a pen or pencil, put it down. If you are typing on the computer, stop typing on the computer. If you are using a voice-to-text or transcription program like Dragon, stop talking.

Get up, and say to your inner child, "Alright, it's play time."

And do something fun:

- Play music and dance around.
- Jump up and down and act silly.
- Go outside in nature and hug a tree.

Do whatever that inner child feels like doing in that moment for the next ten minutes; do it. No matter how silly you feel.

Have fun with your inner child for those ten minutes, and then come back to where you are writing and say, "Okay, it is time now for me to have fun, to write this book and don't you worry, I'll be back in another twenty five minutes," and set that alarm.

When the alarm goes off, get up again and go do what the inner child wants to do for that ten minutes. Rinse and repeat this for your marathon writing time and I guarantee you, you will never experience what people call writer's block.

THE ROADMAP TO BOOK-WRITING SUCCESS

Many people have tried and failed to write a book themselves. The reason that they have experienced this seeming failure is because they just decided to write a book and started writing. Or maybe they even made a contents page for their book and chunked it down and they decided to start writing from chapter one and write forward. The challenge with this is that if chapter one has something that is extremely heavy and you don't want to face it or look at it, it can stop you in your tracks and you will stop writing.

If you are one of those folks who just started without a roadmap, you have started while having no idea where your book was going to start and where it was going to end. You'll just write until you run out of ideas and when you run out of ideas you'll stop. These are the reasons I truly believe anyone who wants to have success in writing a book must start with what we call the *Roadmap to Success*.

"Still Writing..."

If you start without a roadmap, without knowing where your book is going to start and where it will end, you could be writing your book forever. I met a woman years ago at an event where I was speaking. She was asking me tons of questions about book writing. She revealed that she has been working on her book for three years and was still working on it. I suggested that she hire me to help her take her book to completion. She assured me that "she had this" and that she didn't need my support. She was doing fine writing her book on her own.

Months later, I saw her at another event, and I said, "Hey, how's that book going?"

She looked at me and said, "Oh, I'm still writing."

I ran into her again about a year later and I said, "Hey, how's it going with that book?"

She said, "I'm still writing."

I am pretty sure that if I saw that young woman today and asked the same question, I'd get the same answer. This is what can happen when you don't know where your book is going to start and where it's going to end. You may end up writing and writing and writing, and not have any idea when to call the book done. A very important part of getting a book to completion is knowing when to call your book *done*. By done, I mean ready to call it *done for now* and hand it to your editors.

Driving Blind

Writing a book without a roadmap is like driving blind.

If you are in California and you wanted to get to a family event in New York, would you just jump in your car and start driving?

Oh, I think I can take the 405 North to 10 East. I could take 10 East across the United States, and eventually, I think there is the highway that goes up to New York. I'm not sure, but I will figure it out when I get there.

This is driving blind. If I wanted to get from California to New York, back in the day, I would have grabbed a map and I would have mapped my course using a highlighter pen. I would know every highway that I was going to take. Currently, we have systems like navigation programs on our phones or Google Maps to help us get to our destination. Even though we are being led by these systems, we are still not driving blind. When writing a book, driving blind is possibly the worst thing that one can do.

The Roadmap Process — Writing the Book Yourself

Once you've got the subject for your new book, it's time to create your *Roadmap to Success*!

Here's how:

Sit down with a piece of paper and a pencil, ready to write. Now, think of all the stories and elements you want to put into your book. Come up with a short description of these stories or elements and write them down on the blank sheet of paper in no particular order. Just get them onto the paper. Write them all down until you have all of your stories on the paper.

Let me give you an example. If I were writing a life-story book, my list might look something like this:

> The day I was born
> My sister raised me
> My parents' divorce
> Mom's disease
> The day I graduated (barely)
> School was not my forte
> My time in college
> My first true love
> My first marriage
> Finding myself
> The day my son was born
> My divorce

Life as a single dad
How I found my perfect mate
Our relationship Mission Statement
8/8/99 the best day of my life
When you call yourself a relationship expert...
Our first book
How to keep love alive and well
The only thing I can change is me
Ten years and still in love
Here's to the next ten years

Once you have written down all of the stories or elements you will put into your book, go back to your list and put numbers next to them. Number them in the order you'd like to tell the stories, with one being the first story you want to share and the highest number being the last story you want to tell. They do not have to be in the order or the timeframe they happened in, they just need to be in the order you want to share them in.

Now, transfer all of your titles on a new, blank sheet of paper—numbered and in order this time.

Example:

1. The day I was born
2. My parent's divorce
3. Mom's disease
4. My sister raised me

5. School was not my forte
6. The day I graduated (barely)
7. My time in college
8. My first true love
9. My first marriage
10. The day my son was born
11. My divorce
12. Life as a single dad
13. Finding myself
14. How I found my perfect mate
15. 8/8/99 the best day of my life
16. Our relationship Mission Statement
17. When you call yourself a relationship expert…
18. Our first book
19. Ten years and still in love
20. How to keep love alive and well
21. The only thing I can change is me
22. Here's to the next ten years

Once you've completed this process, go the top of your sheet of paper and write ROADMAP on the top of the page.

You have created the majority of your contents page and now you have your *Roadmap to Success*. You will use this roadmap to keep you on course as you navigate the writing of your book. You are ready to start writing now!

There are only two rules to follow to have an effective roadmap experience:

1. **Pick the story or subject on your list that is most juicy for you right now and write that one first.** You see, you don't have to go in order now. You created your roadmap before you started writing. You know where to start and where to end. This allows you to write the stories in any order you wish. It's best to start off with the most exciting or the one that really wants to be written first.

2. **Finish the chapter you are writing before moving onto another chapter.** This keeps you on course and always moving forward in your progress. And, the next thing you know, you'll go to pick another chapter and you'll realize that you have no more chapters to write and you have completed the majority of the book!

Once you've completed all the chapters — in free-form writing, no editing — go to the beginning and read from chapter one all the way through the book. Make any changes you see fit to during this one-time read through.

Once you've completed your one-time read through, write the conclusion chapter to wrap things up.

Once the conclusion is written it's time to write your introduction.

A good introduction includes:

- What the book is about
- Why you wrote it
- What you hope the reader will receive

It's best to write the introduction last, because it should include your experience of writing the book. This cannot be shared until you've finished writing the book.

Now, create the final elements as needed.

Possibilities include:

- Dedication
- Acknowledgments
- Foreword
- About the Author
- Next Steps
- Appendix
- Index

Happy writing!

CHAPTER FIVE

The YouSpeakIt Book Program

YOUR *WHY*

As I previously stated, your *why* for writing your book is incredibly important to know.

Your why is the thing that:

- Pulls you out of bed on the days you'd rather not get up
- Makes you write when you are not in the mood
- Gets you past the excuses and the obstacles

When your why is more important than all of the things that try to take you out, you will find that you keep your appointment, you show up and give your 100 percent until you have your manuscript completed. In this section, I help you discover your why by inviting you to answer these questions, putting as many words as you can in your answers. Let's discover your why together.

Answer these three questions in depth:

1. Why Do You Want to Write This Book?

_____

_____

_____

_____

_____

_____

_____

_____

_____

_____

_____

2. Whom Will Your Book Serve, Inspire, Support, or Motivate?

_____

_____

_____

_____

_____

_____

_____

_____

_____

_____

_____

3. What's the Most Important Thing About Getting Your Book Out of Your Head and Into Print?

_____

_____

_____

_____

_____

_____

_____

_____

_____

_____

_____

_____

_____

How was this process for you?

Have you discovered your why?

Are you seeing whom your book will serve?

Did you take a moment to close your eyes, hand them your book, and see the look on their faces?

During this process, did you take a moment to see them come back to you with tears in their eyes and thank you for writing this book?

All of this is what will keep you writing when you don't want to write. Now that you have written the answers to these questions, during your book-writing process, should you forget what your why is, or whom your book will serve, or what was the most important thing about getting your book out of your head and into print, you can come back, pick up this book, and read the answers to these questions.

Now that you're clearer about your why, let's come up with a why statement for you. This will be one sentence that will remind you why you're writing. It will serve as a powerful tool for you.

Fill in the blanks:

My book will serve, inspire, support, or motivate _____ to/as _____ _____.

Examples:

My book will motivate <u>women</u> to <u>step into their divine feminine and claim their power</u>.

My book will serve <u>the masses</u> as <u>a transformation tool for personal and business success</u>.

My book will inspire <u>entrepreneurs</u> to <u>use their book as a leverage tool to skyrocket their business</u>.

This why statement will help pull you from the ledge anytime you are having a tough time maintaining inspiration to write. You may even want to run this statement in your head all day long, as you remember to do so. I shared previously about affirmative statements and how they can be used to reprogram your mind for good. This is a powerful tool to do that!

YOUR BOOK

Because you have ended up with this book in your hand, I believe you are now discovering that a book is so much more than *just a book*. A book can be a launchpad to your success. A book can be your business card. A book can be something that touches the heart of another. A book can be filled with stories of inspiration. There are so many things a book can be.

What will your book be?

Do You Want to Write the Book Yourself?

At this point, it is very important to answer this question:

Do you want to write the book yourself?

Some of you may be thinking: *Yes. I love to write. I've been writing for years. I've written articles for newspapers.*

Maybe you have even written books before and you just love to write. Great, you will most likely make the time to write. You will do all the things that you will need to get your book done. If this is you, fantastic. If you are a busy entrepreneur, a business owner, a functional medical practitioner, a life coach, a business mentor or a mentor of some sort, now would be a great time to ask yourself if you want to write this book yourself.

Do You Really Have The Time?

Next, ask yourself: *Do I really have the time?*

And more important, ask yourself: *Am I willing to make the time?*

Will you schedule writing time for yourself?

Will you make yourself just as important as everyone else?

Do you feel 100 percent committed to making this happen for you and for your readers?

Will you be able to look at your family members and say, "I don't have time right now; I've got to keep this appointment with myself to write my book."

Do you have the time with your current business commitments, family commitments, and all other time commitments?

If the answer is yes, you are on course to write a book yourself. Take out the calendar right now and schedule the time that you will need to complete your book.

Would You Like Someone Else to Write It for You?

I have spoken all over this country and here's what I have found: Eight out of ten people I have met want to write a book, but less than 1 percent will ever do it. I work with people through my group mentor programs and I do one-on-one mentoring with authors. Over the years, I've asked why their books are still being worked on or abandoned. I have discovered that the number-one reason that people don't complete their book is that they don't have the time. Or, they are not willing to make the time.

Entrepreneurs, functional medical practitioners, mentors, coaches, and people who are being of service to others rarely have the time to sit down and write a book.

So, the question at this point is, would you like to have it done for you?

What if all you had to do was show up to seven phone calls and talk about what you already know?

What if all you had to do was show up and share about what you talk about all day long in your business?

Would this be of interest to you?

HOW THE PROGRAM WORKS

If you would like to have your book done for you, you are not alone. And that is why we have created the YouSpeakIt Book Program. It is for people like you, who are too busy to write their own book. Let me share with you what this program is, and what it includes.

First, we do what we call *The Roadmap Call*. It's about two hours long, and on this call, we get clear about exactly what your book is going to be.

Next come five chapter calls, and the sixth and last call is for the conclusion and introduction. All of these calls are recorded.

Then, the calls are transcribed. We send you the transcription to quickly review.

This is your chance to remove anything you wish you didn't say or to add anything you wish you had said, but forgot.

You'll quickly send the transcription review back to us and we'll move your manuscript into editing.

This is when we transform your manuscript from the spoken word to the written word. We make it sound more like a book *while keeping your voice*. I will say that again because this is something that sets us apart from other companies: We'll make it sound more like a book *while keeping your voice.* You are speaking the book. We are going to take your words, edit them, and polish them up to read well in book form.

How many times have you heard stories about editors coming in and rewording things so much that the author didn't even recognize their own book?

We don't do that. Our editors were untrained and retrained. We want to make sure that when your friends, family, and clients read your book, they hear your voice in their head.

They'll come to you and say, "I could really hear your voice in this book."

That's very important to us.

Once the editing is done, it comes back to you for a quick glance.

You get to read it and say, "Wow, this is good!" or, "Wow, *I'm* good!"

You'll give us the thumbs up to move on, and your manuscript moves to proofreading. Proofreaders *love* to read books and they read them quickly and accurately. Since they're putting a fresh set of eyes on the text, and they haven't seen the manuscript until this point, if there is a comma or period out of place, it will reach up off the page and smack them. Proofreaders are wonderful and we value them very much.

Once the book is proofread, it goes into the production phase, which includes:

Interior layout — This is where we make the document look like a book. We add page numbers, headers, space things out appropriately, and get the file ready so the book can be printed.

Then it's time for your book cover.

Once the layout and cover are completed, we will put your book up for sale on Amazon (using a sister company of Amazon called *CreateSpace*). It's a print-on-demand company. Working with them makes it so you never have to lick a stamp or ship books yourself. When someone buys your book on Amazon, CreateSpace will make the book and ship it to the customer for you, and you get a commission on the book sale. Of course, you'll make the most money from the books you sell out of your hand or at events. Never having to ship a book yourself is a luxury and it's worth it to have your book for sale on the number-one book retail site in the world.

Once your book is set up with the printer, we'll ship your first twenty books to you at no cost. Those first twenty books are included in the program.

Some people wonder why we chose twenty as the number of books to include.

Every other company that has book packages for clients has a minimum purchase they build into the program. They make you pre-purchase five hundred copies at ten dollars each. When they do this, it bumps up the price of the package, which is unfair to you, because it's an additional five thousand dollars.

Plus, what brand-new author knows what to do with five hundred books?

We want to make sure you don't have boxes of books that you overpaid for sitting around. We will send you the first twenty (included) and you can give those to friends and family while you wait for an order of exactly how many books you would like to purchase. If you want to order an additional twenty-five, fifty, or even a hundred books, you buy them at the wholesale cost, plus shipping. The price per book is the same whether you order one or one thousand copies — it's just wholesale cost, plus shipping. The book cost is based on the final page count and book dimensions.

Books in the YouSpeakIt Book Program fit a specific set of criteria. They're 15,000–25,000-word manuscripts (which come out to be between 120 and 140 pages). The finished dimensions are 5.25 x 8 inches. This is the perfect size for a book in the current market.

When you hand a book this size to someone, they think to themselves: *I can read this.*

Plus, you don't have to come up with tons and tons of information for the book. You just show up and allow us to guide you through the process with grace and ease.

How does that sound?

One thing we've learned from being in the book business for all these years is this: a book that is put off until later is rarely if *ever* written.

Are you ready to get your book done at warp speed?

I like to say, "The only good book is one I can hold in my hands. The only *perfect* book is one that's done!"

The people who need to read your book are waiting, so, let's get your book started right away.

Do you want to find out more about the YouSpeakIt program?

Do you have a few questions you'd like answered before getting started?

Are you ready now to make the commitment and get started right away?

If you answered yes to any of these questions, follow the instructions in the Next Steps section at the end of this book to get more information and a complimentary strategy session.

Conclusion

This has been quite a journey. In this book, I have shared with you what the world's greatest business card is and why most people don't ever get their book to completion. I shared about traditional publishing versus self-publishing. I've shared with you tips and ways to write your book if you want to write it yourself, and I've told you about the YouSpeakIt Book Program if you don't want to write the book yourself.

It has been my pleasure to share with you all of this information that I have gained over the last fifteen years. I know what it's like to want to write and not be able to. I know what it's like to face obstacles and excuses. I know what it's like to write a book, and I know what it's like to complete one. I have experienced all these things and more. I've also experienced much success in creating bestselling books for myself and others. I've been blessed enough to help thousands of people over the years to write their books, to grow their businesses, to share their mission and their message with the world. It is my great pleasure and I love what I do.

If after reading this book you want to write the book yourself, I encourage you to take what you've learned in this book and get started right away. Pull out your calendar. Make those writing appointments. Make your writing as important as you make everyone else. Make yourself, your business, and your readers as important as you make everybody else. If you have decided that you would like support, and you do not want to write the book yourself, I encourage you to contact us immediately so that we can get started.

If there is one thing that I have learned and know for sure, it's that the only good book is one that is completed. And the only perfect book is one that I can hold in my hand and read. A book that's put off until later, or Someday, is never written. Procrastination will kill a good book every time.

If you are feeling inspired to write your book, now is the time. Take the action, get started, and, happy writing!

Next Steps

You've read all the pros and cons of writing a book. Now is the time to make the decision about which form of writing best fits your book.

Which will get your book to your readers or potential clients as soon as possible?

What did you decide?

Are you going to write the book yourself?

If so, I suggest using our *Bake Your Book Home Study Course* to guide you through the process. Find out more at www.BakeYourBookNow.com.

Would you like to write a book without ever having to put pen to paper?

If you have this book in your hand right now, someone who cares about you has given it to you. We want to know who that was.

Please fill in their name here, so you can remember when we ask:

_____

Next, go to meetme.so/keithleons and book a date and time in our calendar for your strategy session and to find out more about the YouSpeakIt Book Program.

Have You Already Written a Book?

We offer every service you need to turn your manuscript into a book—including:

- Manuscript evaluation
- Editing
- Proofreading
- Interior layout
- Cover design
- Print-on-demand
- Kindle setup
- Amazon book page setup
- Promotional programs

We have everything it takes to get your book into the hands of those who are eagerly awaiting your story!

We look forward to working with you to get your mission, message, or story out to the world.

To order books published by our company, or by our self-published clients, go to LeonSmithPublishing.com and click on any of the book covers you see there.

About the Author

After overcoming numerous personal obstacles, including extreme poverty, a broken home, family illnesses and deaths, severe bullying, drug addiction, and even attempting suicide, Keith Leon S went on to become a multiple bestselling author, book publisher, and book mentor. Now well known as "The Book Guy," Keith and his wife, Maura, co-authored the book, *The Seven Steps to Successful Relationships*, acclaimed by bestselling authors John Gray and Terry Cole-Whittaker, and Keith authored the bestselling book, *Who Do You Think You Are? Discover the Purpose of Your Life*, with a foreword by *Chicken Soup for The Soul's* Jack Canfield.

Keith's writing has also been featured in Warren Henningsen's *If I Can You Can*, Jennifer McLean's *The Big Book of You*, Justin Sachs' *The Power of Persistence and Ultimate Business Mastery*, Ron Prasad's *Welcome to Your Life*; and many other books, including *The Bake Your Book Program: How to Finish Your Book Fast and Serve it Up HOT* and his latest bestseller, *YOU Make a Difference: 50 Heart-Centered Entrepreneurs Share Their Stories of Inspiration and Transformation*.

Keith has appeared on popular radio and television broadcasts, including *The Rolonda Watts Show* and *The John Kerwin Show*, and his work has been covered by *Inc.* magazine, *LA Weekly*; *The Valley Reporter*; *Healthy, Wealthy 'n' Wise*; *The Minneapolis-St. Paul Star Tribune*; *The Maryland Herald-Mail*; *The Huffington Post*; and *Succeed Magazine*.

As a professional speaker, book mentor, and a developer and facilitator of transformational seminars, Keith is a recognized expert at helping authors get their book out of their heads and into print. He has helped numerous authors reach bestseller status, get free press, and get booked to speak on the big stage. Keith has spoken at events that included Jack Canfield, Neale Donald Walsch, Dr. John Demartini, Lee Brower, Christine Comaford-Lynch, Joel Bauer, Armand Morin, Paul Martinelli, Barbara De Angelis, Dr. John Gray, Dr.

Michael Bernard Beckwith, Alex Mandossian, T. Harv Eker, Adam Markel, and Marianne Williamson.

Keith's passion is teaching people how to go from first thought to bestseller and how to create what he calls *The World's Greatest Business Card*. He does this through his book-writing programs and by providing any and all book services writers need to get their books completed and out to the world.

Testimonials

Here's What Our Happy Authors Are Saying

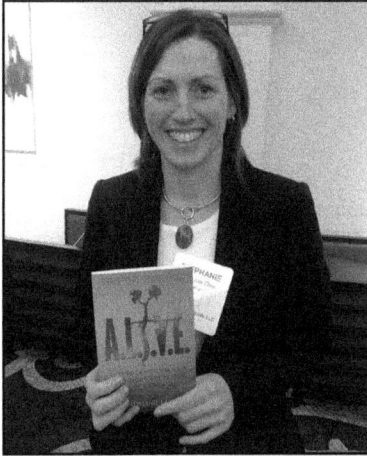

"If you can talk about your business, you can do this process. The *YouSpeakIt* Book Program is both seamless and amazingly easy."

— Stephanie J. Clark, DC, Author of *A.L.I.V.E.*
How to Transform Your Cells and Yourself
from Disease to Wellness

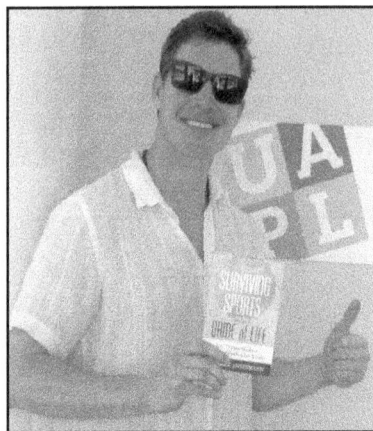

"It is a rare opportunity to work with such a genuine leader in the publishing business like Keith Leon. My favorite aspect of the YouSpeakIt Book Program was getting out of my analytical ego-head and speaking the truth from my heart intelligence. There is no other authentic process like this."

— Frederick Entenmann, Bestselling Author of
*Surviving Sports and the Game of Life: Your Holistic
Guide to Achieving World-Class Results*

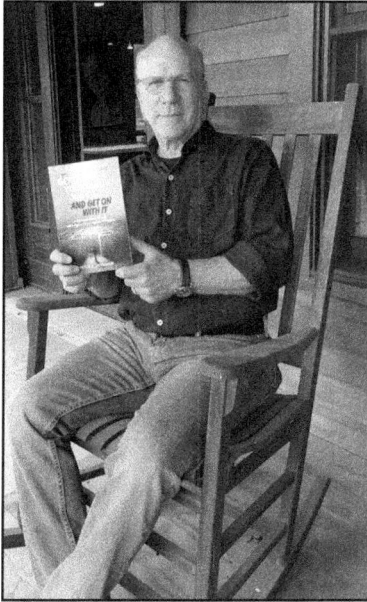

"Thanks so much to the YouSpeakIt publishing team. This journey has been amazing! I'm so excited with my book and now using it to build my practice."
— Peter Heymann, Author of *Get Out of Your Own Way… and Get On With It: A Practical Guide to Stop Self-Judgment and Negative Thinking*

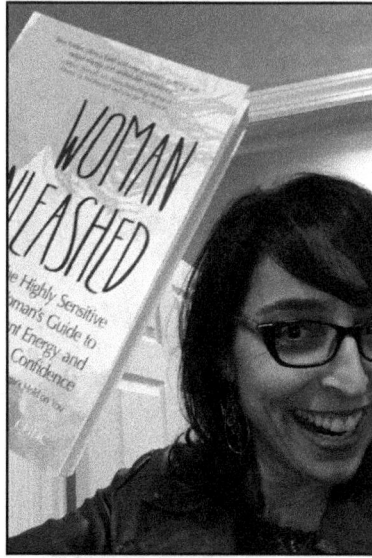

"Check out what one former client said about my book: *'Jenn! So good to hear from you. I am halfway through your book. It's been a great companion this past month. I can absolutely hear your voice in very page.'* Thank you, YouSpeakIt team members."

— Jenn Edden, Author of *Woman Unleashed:*
The Highly Sensitive Woman's Guide to Radiant Energy,
Unstoppable Confidence, and a 21-Day Plan to Kick
Sugar's Hold on You

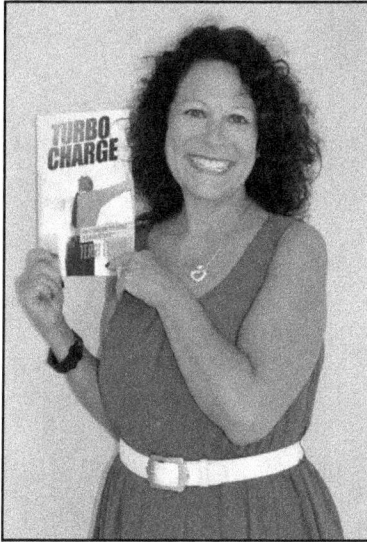

"This is the easiest writing a book has ever been for me!"

> — Terri Levine, Business Mentoring Expert and Author of *Turbo Charge: How to Transform Your Business as a Heart-Repreneur*

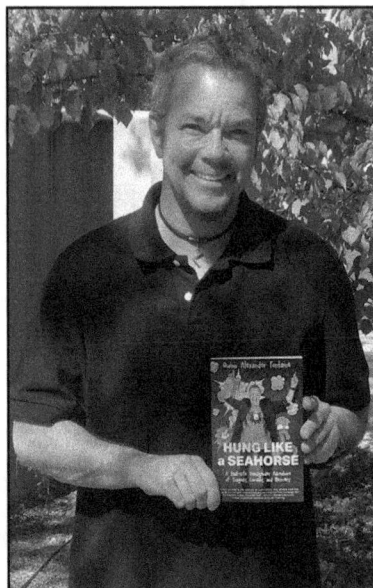

"I loved every aspect of working with the YouSpeakIt book process. The entire team helped me overcome the fears and obstacles of writing my first book. They truly helped me birth this baby! I am so grateful for their guidance, love, and support. Without them, the book never would have been written."

– Quinn Alexander, Actor, Comedian, and Author of
Hung Like a Seahorse: A Real-Life Transgender Adventure
of Tragedy, Comedy, and Recovery

"I had been putting off creating my book for years until I finally found Keith Leon, 'The Book Guy.' He taught me a clever way to create a book without having to write it myself. And through the process, I'm meeting inspiring leaders and expanding my network of potential perfect customers. Keith always goes way beyond what I expect in terms of supporting me in the process. He really is 'The Book Guy.' I cannot sing him enough praise."

— Julia D. Stege, Marketing Expert and
Author of *The Magical Marketing Attraction Planning Workbook*

"Thank you, YouSpeakIt Publishing, for helping me complete my book. I would have never gotten it done without you. I appreciate you, and you are making a huge impact. Don't forget that."

— David W. Adams, DC, Author of *Don't Just Be Alive...LIVE! Naturally Restoring Your Maximum Human Potential*

"Having and using *The World's Greatest Business Card* will change your life and your business forever!"

— Ronny K. Prasad, Bestselling Author of *Welcome To Your Life: Simple Insights for Your Inspiration and Empowerment*

"Thanks to Keith Leon, 'The Book Guy,' for helping me to write this book. He took something I thought was going to be hard and made it easy. I cannot thank him enough for his mentorship and friendship."

— Edward Chauvin, DC, Author of *I'm Worried Sick About My Health: How to Get and Stay Healthy Without Spending a Fortune*

"Keith and Maura Leon of the YouSpeakIt Publishing have given tremendous help throughout the process of writing this book. I didn't know where I would start or where I would end. They made it easy for me."

— Ron Nottingham, Author of *The Gift of Leadership: How to Coach Your Team to More Productive and Efficient Outcomes*

"I love this book cover. The cover artist was tapped into my higher self, for sure. It's perfect!"
— Kat Wells, Author of *There's Got to Be Something More: Powerful Tools for Creating and Loving the Life You Came to Live*

"I know I am not a writer just yet, but I'm in training with the best teachers I could ever pray for: the team at YouSpeakIt Publishing. What an honor it is to be working with all of you."
— Tonijean Kulpinski, CBHC, BCHP, AADP, Board-Certified Holistic Drugless Practitioner

"I want to thank you for being such a big part of my life. Because you believed in me, with your help, not only did I write a book—it's a bestseller!"
– Karen Kan, Physician, Healer, and Bestselling Author of *Guide to Healing Chronic Pain: A Holistic Approach*

"Doing the Amazon Bestseller Book Program with YouSpeakIt is the greatest thing I have done for my business in years. I started using my bestselling book as a giveaway at my talks, and my closing ratio is through the roof."
— Trevor Botts, Author of *The Hidden Hormone Solution: Discover the Secret to Health and Vitality at Any Age*

"Keith, Maura, and their team have definitely made this process easy. I can't emphasize that enough. I have been working on this for *five* years! You managed to get me through it in less than one year."
— Danna J. Olivo, Business Growth Strategist and
Author of *MarketAtomy: What to Expect
When Expecting a Business*

"This is a comforting and beautiful process. Your methodology of allowing and creating a safe place is an experience in which I can truly trust the process, be at peace with what is, and celebrate the opening."
— Martha Hackett, MD, Soon-to-be Published
YouSpeakIt Author

"I have enjoyed my time on the content calls with Sunni. He is so helpful. I am very pleased with the process so far. I trust it, and I cannot wait to see the final product!"
— Carmen Keith, MD, Soon-to-be Published
YouSpeakIt Author

"Thank you, YouSpeakIt Book Program, for making the book creation journey so smooth."
— Jean-Ronel Corbier, Author of *From Autism to
Alzheimer's and Everything in Between: How to Fix the
Brain Using the Restoration Model*

"The YouSpeakIt Book program is incredible, to say the least. I'm not a writer though I can write and sometimes enjoy it, but had I *not* taken the leap into this program, I *still* would not have a book. Thank you, Keith for the gentle nudge to get me to take action to get this book happening! I can't recommend this program enough. Such a beautiful process and a fun way to get your book from thought to print! Thank you so much!"

— Marjean Holden, International Trainer, Actress, and Author of *The Power of the Goddess: A Woman's Journey to Awakening, Cultivating, and Sustaining Her Power*

"Using a strategy learned from Keith Leon, I presold over $3,000 in books at an event before my book was even completed. Using my book as a business card the exact way Keith taught me got me booked as a speaker at a Tony Robbins event!"

— Jessica Brace, Video Marketing Mentor and Author of *Ready, Set, GO Make A Video: 101 YouTube Ideas for Your Business*

"Working with Keith Leon has been a dream come true for me. I started writing my book some time before working with Keith. I used to think writing a book was hard, but now I've seen how easy it can be. It's all about putting together a bunch of baby steps. One step at a time adds up pretty quickly to a finished book."

— Melanie Eatherton, Speaker, Author of *The 7 Minute Mirror: Reflection – Re-Vision – Results*

"I highly recommend YouSpeakIt Publishing! I am grateful for all they did for me to assist in getting my book to the International Best Seller List."

— Warren Henningsen, Author of *If I Can You Can: Insights of an Average Man*

"I was so excited to receive the hard copy books today. I can't believe I actually got a book done—I always wanted to, but without the help of your group, it would still be a pie-in-the-sky hope!"

— Jean Golden-Tevald, DO, Author of *Hope and Healing: Ultimately What You Need From Your Doctor*